Of Seditions And Troubles

Francis Bacon

Kessinger Publishing's Rare Reprints

Thousands of Scarce and Hard-to-Find Books on These and other Subjects!

- Americana
- Ancient Mysteries
- Animals
- Anthropology
- Architecture
- Arts
- Astrology
- Bibliographies
- Biographies & Memoirs
- Body, Mind & Spirit
- Business & Investing
- Children & Young Adult
- Collectibles
- Comparative Religions
- Crafts & Hobbies
- Earth Sciences
- Education
- Ephemera
- Fiction
- Folklore
- Geography
- Health & Diet
- History
- Hobbies & Leisure
- Humor
- Illustrated Books
- Language & Culture
- Law
- Life Sciences
- Literature
- Medicine & Pharmacy
- Metaphysical
- Music
- Mystery & Crime
- Mythology
- Natural History
- Outdoor & Nature
- Philosophy
- Poetry
- Political Science
- Science
- Psychiatry & Psychology
- Reference
- Religion & Spiritualism
- Rhetoric
- Sacred Books
- Science Fiction
- Science & Technology
- Self-Help
- Social Sciences
- Symbolism
- Theatre & Drama
- Theology
- Travel & Explorations
- War & Military
- Women
- Yoga
- *Plus Much More!*

We kindly invite you to view our catalog list at:
http://www.kessinger.net

THIS ARTICLE WAS EXTRACTED FROM THE BOOK:

Essays or Counsels, Civil and Moral

BY THIS AUTHOR:

Francis Bacon

ISBN 1564592286

READ MORE ABOUT THE BOOK AT OUR WEB SITE:

http://www.kessinger.net

OR ORDER THE COMPLETE
BOOK FROM YOUR FAVORITE STORE

ISBN 1564592286

Because this article has been extracted from a parent book, it may have non-pertinent text at the beginning or end of it.

OF SEDITIONS AND TROUBLES   51

XV.—OF SEDITIONS AND TROUBLES

SHEPHERDS of people had need know the calendars of tempests in state, which are commonly greatest when things grow to equality ; as natural tempests are greatest

* Consistent with reason and justice.

BACON'S ESSAYS

about the *Æquinoctia,** and as there are certain hollow blasts of wind and secret swellings of seas before a tempest, so are there in states :—

> ——*Ille etiam cæcos instare tumultus*
> *Sæpe monet, fraudesque et operta tumescere bella.* †

Libels and licentious discourses against the state, when they are frequent and open ; and in like sort false news, often running up and down, to the disadvantage of the state, and hastily embraced, are amongst the signs of troubles. Virgil, giving the pedigree of Fame, saith she was sister to the giants :—

> *Illam Terra parens, irâ irritata Deorum,*
> *Extremam (ut perhibent) Cœo Enceladoque sororem*
> *Progenuit.* ‡

As if fames were the relics of seditions past ; but they are no less indeed the preludes of seditions to come. Howsoever he noteth it right, that seditious tumults and seditious fames differ no more but as brother and sister, masculine and feminine ; especially if it come to that, that the best actions of a state, and the most plausible, and which ought to give greatest contentment, are taken in ill sense, and traduced : for that shows the envy great, as Tacitus saith, *Conflatâ magna invidiâ, seu bene, seu male, gesta premunt.* § Neither doth it follow, that because these fames are a sign of troubles, that the suppressing of them with too much severity should be a remedy of troubles ; for the despising of them many times checks them best, and the going about

---

* The periods of the Equinoxes.

† " He often warns, too, that secret revolt is impending, that treachery and open warfare are ready to burst forth."

‡ " Mother Earth, exasperated at the wrath of the Deities, produced her, as they tell, a last birth, a sister to *the Giants* Cœus and Enceladus."

§ " Great public odium once excited, his deeds, whether good or whether bad, cause his downfall."

OF SEDITIONS AND TROUBLES   53

to stop them doth but make a wonder long-lived. Also that kind of obedience, which Tacitus speaketh of, is to be held suspected: *Erant in officio, sed tamen qui mallent mandata imperantium interpretari, quam exequi ;* * disputing, excusing, cavilling upon mandates and directions, is a kind of shaking off the yoke, and assay of disobedience ; especially if in those disputings they which are for the direction speak fearfully and tenderly, and those that are against it audaciously.

Also, as Machiavel noteth well, when princes, that ought to be common parents, make themselves as a party, and lean to a side; it is, as a boat that is overthrown by uneven weight on the one side ; as was well seen in the time of Henry the Third of France ; for first himself entered league for the extirpation of the Protestants, and presently after the same league was turned upon himself : for when the authority of princes is made but an accessary to a cause, and that there be other bands that tie faster than the band of sovereignty, kings begin to be put almost out of possession.

Also, when discords, and quarrels, and factions, are carried openly and audaciously, it is a sign the reverence of government is lost ; for the motions of the greatest persons in a government ought to be as the motions of the planets under *primum mobile,* † according to the old opinion, which is, that every of them is carried swiftly by the highest motion, and softly in their own motion ; and therefore, when great ones in their own particular motion move violently, and as Tacitus expresseth it well, *liberius quam ut imperantium meminissent,* ‡ it is a sign the orbs are out of frame : for reverence is that

---

* " They attended to their duties, but still, as preferring rather to discuss the commands of their rulers, than to obey them."

† " The primary motive power." He alludes to an imaginary centre of gravitation, or central body, which was supposed to set all the other heavenly bodies in motion.

‡ " Too freely to remember their own rulers."

54 BACON'S ESSAYS

wherewith princes are girt from God, who threateneth the dissolving thereof : *Solvam cingula regum.**

So when any of the four pillars of government are mainly shaken or weakened (which are religion, justice, counsel, and treasure), men had need to pray for fair weather. But let us pass from this part of predictions (concerning which, nevertheless, more light may be taken from that which followeth), and let us speak first of the materials of seditions ; then of the motives of them ; and thirdly of the remedies.

Concerning the materials of seditions, it is a thing well to be considered ; for the surest way to prevent seditions (if the times do bear it) is to take away the matter of them ; for if there be fuel prepared, it is hard to tell whence the spark shall come that shall set it on fire. The matter of seditions is of two kinds ; much poverty and much discontentment. It is certain, so many overthrown estates, so many votes for troubles. Lucan noteth well the state of Rome before the civil war :—

> *Hinc usura vorax, rapidumque in tempore fœnus,*
> *Hinc concussa fides, et multis utile bellum.†*

This same *multis utile bellum,* ‡ is an assured and infallible sign of a state disposed to seditions and troubles ; and if this poverty and broken estate in the better sort be joined with a want and necessity in the mean people, the danger is imminent and great: for the rebellions of the belly are the worst. As for discontentments, they are in the politic body like to humours in the natural, which are apt to gather a preternatural heat and to inflame ; and let no prince measure the danger of them by this, whether they be just or unjust : for that were

---

* " I will unloose the girdles of the kings."

† " Hence devouring usury, and interest accumulating in lapse of time,—hence shaken credit, and warfare, profitable to the many."

‡ " Warfare profitable to the many."

OF SEDITIONS AND TROUBLES 55

to imagine people to be too reasonable, who do often spurn at their own good; nor yet by this, whether the griefs whereupon they rise be in fact great or small; for they are the most dangerous discontentments where the fear is greater than the feeling: *Dolendi modus, timendi non item:* * besides, in great oppressions, the same things that provoke the patience, do withal mate † the courage; but in fears it is not so; neither let any prince or state be secure concerning discontentments, because they have been often, or have been long, and yet no peril hath ensued: for as it is true that every vapour or fume doth not turn into a storm, so it is nevertheless true that storms, though they blow over divers times, yet may fall at last; and, as the Spanish proverb noteth well, *The cord breaketh at the last by the weakest pull.*

The causes and motives of seditions are, innovation in religion, taxes, alteration of laws and customs, breaking of privileges, general oppression, advancement of unworthy persons, strangers, dearths, disbanded soldiers, factions grown desperate; and whatsoever in offending people joineth and knitteth them in a common cause.

For the remedies, there may be some general preservatives, whereof we will speak: as for the just cure, it must answer to the particular disease; and so be left to counsel rather than rule.

The first remedy, or prevention, is to remove, by all means possible, that material cause of sedition whereof we spake, which is, want and poverty in the estate: ‡ to which purpose serveth the opening and well-balancing of trade; the cherishing of manufactures; the banishing of idleness; the repressing of waste and excess, by sumptuary laws; the improvement and husbanding of

---

* " To grief there is a limit, not so to fear."
† " Check," or " daunt."
‡ The state.

BACON'S ESSAYS

the soil; the regulating of prices of things vendible; the moderating of taxes and tributes, and the like. Generally, it is to be foreseen that the population of a kingdom (especially if it be not mown down by wars) do not exceed the stock of the kingdom which should maintain them: neither is the population to be reckoned only by number; for a smaller number, that spend more and earn less, do wear out an estate sooner than a greater number that live lower and gather more: therefore the multiplying of nobility, and other degrees of quality, in an over proportion to the common people, doth speedily bring a state to necessity; and so doth likewise an overgrown clergy, for they bring nothing to the stock; and, in like manner, when more are bred scholars than preferments can take off.

It is likewise to be remembered, that, forasmuch as the increase of any estate must be upon the foreigner (for whatsoever is somewhere gotten is somewhere lost), there be but three things which one nation selleth unto another; the commodity, as nature yieldeth it; the manufacture; and the vecture, or carriage; so that, if these three wheels go, wealth will flow as in a spring tide. And it cometh many times to pass, that, *materiam superabit opus,** that the work and carriage is more worth than the material, and enricheth a state more: as is notably seen in the Low Countrymen, who have the best mines above ground in the world.

Above all things, good policy is to be used, that the treasure and moneys in a state be not gathered into few hands; for, otherwise, a state may have a great stock, and yet starve: and money is like muck,† not good except it be spread. This is done chiefly by suppressing, or, at least, keeping a strait hand upon the devouring trades of usury, engrossing great pasturages, and the like.

* " The workmanship will surpass the material."—Ovid.
† Manure.

OF SEDITIONS AND TROUBLES

For removing discontentments, or, at least, the danger of them, there is in every state (as we know) two portions of subjects, the nobles and the commonalty. When one of these is discontent, the danger is not great; for common people are of slow motion, if they be not excited by the greater sort; and the greater sort are of small strength, except the multitude be apt and ready to move of themselves: then is the danger, when the greater sort do but wait for the troubling of the waters amongst the meaner, that then they may declare themselves. The poets feign that the rest of the gods would have bound Jupiter; which he hearing of, by the counsel of Pallas, sent for Briareus, with his hundred hands, to come in to his aid: an emblem, no doubt, to show how safe it is for monarchs to make sure of the goodwill of common people.

To give moderate liberty for griefs and discontentments to evaporate (so it be without too great insolency or bravery), is a safe way: for he that turneth the humours back, and maketh the wound bleed inwards, endangereth malign ulcers and pernicious imposthumations.

The part of Epimetheus might well become Prometheus, in the case of discontentments, for there is not a better provision against them. Epimetheus, when griefs and evils flew abroad, at last shut the lid, and kept Hope in the bottom of the vessel. Certainly, the politic and artificial nourishing and entertaining of hopes, and carrying men from hopes to hopes, is one of the best antidotes against the poison of discontentments: and it is a certain sign of a wise government and proceeding, when it can hold men's hearts by hopes, when it cannot by satisfaction; and when it can handle things in such manner as no evil shall appear so peremptory but that it hath some outlet of hope; which is the less hard to do, because both particular persons and factions are apt

58   BACON'S ESSAYS

enough to flatter themselves, or at least to brave that which they believe not.

Also the foresight and prevention, that there be no likely or fit head whereunto discontented persons may resort, and under whom they may join, is a known, but an excellent point of caution. I understand a fit head to be one that hath greatness and reputation, that hath confidence with the discontented party, and upon whom they turn their eyes, and that is thought discontented in his own particular : which kind of persons are either to be won and reconciled to the state, and that in a fast and true manner ; or to be fronted with some other of the same party that may oppose them, and so divide the reputation. Generally, the dividing and breaking of all factions and combinations that are adverse to the state, and setting them at distance, or, at least, distrust amongst themselves, is not one of the worst remedies ; for it is a desperate case, if those that hold with the proceeding of the state be full of discord and faction, and those that are against it be entire and united.

I have noted, that some witty and sharp speeches, which have fallen from princes, have given fire to seditions. Cæsar did himself infinite hurt in that speech—*Sylla nescivit litteras, non potuit dictare;* * for it did utterly cut off that hope which men had entertained, that he would at one time or other give over his dictatorship. Galba undid himself by that speech, *Legi a se militem, non emi;* † for it put the soldiers out of hope of the donative. Probus, likewise, by that speech, *Si vixero, non opus erit amplius Romano imperio militibus;* ‡ a speech of great despair for the soldiers, and many the like. Surely princes had need in tender matters and

---

* " Sylla did not know his letters, *and so* he could not dictate."
† " That soldiers were levied by him and not bought."
‡ " If I live, there shall no longer be need of soldiers in the Roman empire."

OF ATHEISM

59

ticklish times to beware what they say, especially in these short speeches, which fly abroad like darts, and are thought to be shot out of their secret intentions ; for as for large discourses, they are flat things, and not so much noted.

Lastly, let princes, against all events, not be without some great person, one or rather more, of military valour, near unto them, for the repressing of seditions in their beginnings ; for without that, there useth to be more trepidation in court upon the first breaking out of troubles than were fit ; and the state runneth the danger of that which Tacitus saith : *Atque is habitus animorum fuit, ut pessimum facinus auderent pauci, plures vellent, omnes paterentur :* * but let such military persons be assured, and well reputed of, rather than factious and popular ; holding also good correspondence with the other great men in the state, or else the remedy is worse than the disease.

CPSIA information can be obtained
at www.ICGtesting.com
Printed in the USA
LVRC021354200319
611251LV00001B/24